Bath.
An Adumbration in Rhyme

By John Matthews

A Critical Edition for Readers of Jane Austen

Edited by

Ben Wiebracht
Josephine Chan
Carolyn Engargiola
Macy Maurer Levin
Sophia Romagnoli
Kate Snyder
Lauren Stoneman
Varsha Venkatram

PIXELIA PUBLISHING

Bath: An Adumbration in Rhyme. A Critical Edition for Readers of Jane Austen

First Edition

ISBN: 978-1-7370330-1-1
Published by Pixelia Publishing
pixeliapublishing.org
Cover design: Macy Maurer Levin
Cover image: "The Interior of the Pump Room, Bath," John Claude Nattes, 1804. Rijksmuseum, Amsterdam. Public domain.
Font: Garamond

Forgotten Contemporaries of Jane Austen

Volume I. Bath: An Adumbration in Rhyme

Series Editor:

Ben Wiebracht

CONTENTS

Acknowledgments i
An Introduction to the Series ii
Portraits of John Matthews and Jane Austen vi
Original Title Page viii

Introduction 1
    Biographical Essay: John Matthews (1755–1826) 1
    Contextual Essay: The Bath Satire 9
    Bibliography 22
    Further Reading 25
    A Chronology of John Matthews and Jane Austen 26
    A Note on the Text 28

Bath: An Adumbration in Rhyme 30

ACKNOWLEDGMENTS

We wish to thank, first of all, LiYuan Byrne, Ariana Desai, Ava Giles, Gage Miles, Oscar Steinhardt, and Alexandria Thomas. They were our co-authors for the article "A Day in Catherine Morland's Bath," published January 2021 on the blog *Jane Austen's World*. That article, which reintroduced the public to this poem, was the work of the students and teacher of "Advanced Topics: Love Stories," a senior-level course at Stanford Online High School. Some students stayed on to create this book, but the others still helped lay the foundation for it with their work on the article.

We are extraordinarily grateful to Vic Sanborn, editor of *Jane Austen's World*, for believing in this project when it was simply an idea in an email from a stranger (though a friend now). Ms. Sanborn not only published our article on her platform; she visited our class to share her expertise and offered encouragement and practical support at every stage of the project. She also introduced us to Tony Grant, contributor to *Jane Austen's World* and a highly knowledgeable tour guide based in London. Mr. Grant visited our class as well and enriched our understanding of Georgian Bath.

Henry Connor, medical historian and author of an excellent article on John Matthews, was very generous with his time and knowledge. David Nunnery, an English teacher at Stanford OHS and a scholar specializing in the eighteenth century, shed light on several points of Georgian culture. Shaun Regan, an expert on Christopher Anstey and Georgian resort satires, lent a careful eye to the manuscript and improved it in numerous ways. The Royal College of Physicians made available to us records from Matthews' time as a Fellow of that institution: we especially thank archivist Felix Lancashire for sorting through those records on our behalf.

Last but not least, Thomas Hendrickson, Latin and English teacher at Stanford OHS and founder of Pixelia Publishing, guided us through the nitty-gritty details of publication (and helped us translate the Latin passages we encountered). This book would not have made it across the finish line without his help; indeed, it would not have even made it to the starting line, for it was Dr. Hendrickson who first proposed the idea of expanding our article on "Bath: An Adumbration in Rhyme" into a critical edition.

FORGOTTEN CONTEMPORARIES OF JANE AUSTEN

AN INTRODUCTION TO THE SERIES

The 2005 film adaptation of *Pride and Prejudice*, starring Kiera Knightley, had a special ending for its American release. The scene takes place on a torch-lit balcony at Pemberley. Presumably it is the wedding night of Elizabeth and Darcy. No longer bound by the formalities of courtship, husband and wife are in a moderate state of dishabille, seated cross-legged and facing each other. They banter about what Mr. Darcy will call Elizabeth now that they are married – whether "goddess divine" or "my pearl" or, Darcy playfully suggests, "Mrs. Darcy" when he is feeling cross. No, replies Elizabeth; he may only call her "Mrs. Darcy" when he is "perfectly and incandescently happy." Darcy then murmurs "Mrs. Darcy" no fewer than five times as he kisses her brow, her cheek, her nose. The camera never moves from the lovers; instead it zooms in closer and closer, until their faces fill the frame as they lean in for one last, perfect kiss.

 This, on the other hand, is the ending Jane Austen wrote:

> With the Gardiners, they were always on the most intimate terms. Darcy, as well as Elizabeth, really loved them; and they were both ever sensible of the warmest gratitude towards the

persons who, by bringing her into Derbyshire, had been the means of uniting them.

Those who have only read the novel once may need to be reminded who the Gardiners are. In short, they are Elizabeth's favorite aunt and uncle: a likeable, intelligent couple, but certainly minor characters. And yet, here they are at the curtain call, sharing center stage with the hero and heroine themselves. Take the final chapter as a whole, and the stage becomes more crowded. We learn how the Darcys deal with their difficult relatives the Wickhams. We learn that Elizabeth is fast friends with her new sister-in-law, and that the Bingleys have settled near Pemberley. Even Kitty, the most marginal of the Bennet sisters, gets a paragraph: apparently she lives with the Darcys much of the year.

The difference between the two endings boils down to this. In the 21st-century ending, the one meant to appeal to modern American tastes, the central couple is alone, perfectly fulfilled in each other. Their faces dominate the screen; their names echo in our ears. In Austen's ending, the central couple is integrated into a community. Their lives are interwoven with other lives – so much so that the final sentence focuses not on the Darcys' love for each other (though that is present, a steady undercurrent), but on their love for, of all people, the Gardiners.

This series – *Forgotten Contemporaries of Jane Austen* – strives to see Austen in the same way that Austen herself saw Elizabeth and Darcy: not balconied, not high up and alone, but at ground-level and in a broader context. It will do this by recovering some of the Gardiners of her literary world: writers whose work receives little attention today, but who can nevertheless enrich our understanding of Austen and her novels.

In selecting works for this series, we are guided by four criteria.

- First, the work cannot be available in any other modern edition. In a series focused on minor writers, this is not much of a limitation: there are thousands of titles from Austen's time buried in university archives and academic databases that have been neglected for decades if not centuries. This series, of course, can recover only a tiny sliver of that material, but a sliver is better than nothing –

much better, if it piques readers' curiosity about what else might be out there.

- Second, the work must treat subjects that directly concerned Jane Austen and are prominent in her novels. In this inaugural volume, that subject is Bath: the city Austen knew best and wrote about most. In most cases, the work will also represent a literary tradition that influenced her. Austen cut her teeth as a writer by parodying the conventions and genres of her day. To fully appreciate her humor and originality, then, we can't stop at her novels: we have to read what she was reading. The tradition exemplified here is that of the "Bath satire," a tradition Austen both built upon and challenged in *Northanger Abbey* and *Persuasion*.

- Third, the work must be relatively short. This is to enable instructors to assign it as part of a unit or class on Jane Austen. Lest cost become a barrier, students (or anyone else) can download a free e-text of each volume in this series at pixeliapublishing.org.

- Finally, while we do not presume to be publishing forgotten masterpieces, the work must have merit in its own right. We are interested in recovering the Gardiners of Austen's era, not the Collinses, and we believe we offer the reader a Gardiner in John Matthews.

At the core of each volume in this series is a richly annotated text. Whereas most critical editions relegate the notes to the foot of the page or the back of the book, we opt for a side-by-side layout, with the text on the even page and the notes on the odd. This approach makes notes easier to locate and leaves room for ampler commentary. On odd pages readers will find not only historical and cultural context, but images and connections to Austen's works as well. Each volume also includes a biographical essay and a contextual essay. The biographical essay tells the story of the author's life, showing parallels with Austen's life along the way. The contextual essay introduces the reader to the genres, debates, and fashions with which the work is engaged, and explains how they figured into Austen's career.

We are launching this series with a varied audience in mind. Academics will value the rigorous and original scholarship that is the foundation of these volumes. Lovers of Austen, whether associated with academia or not, will appreciate the direct links we draw between the texts and authors we feature and Austen herself. They will also appreciate the accessibility of our commentary, which avoids jargon and attempts to speak as directly as possible to the typical reader – the same reader Austen herself addressed. Finally, teachers and students, particularly high-school students, will be inspired to know that the volume they are reading was researched, designed, and edited in large part by other high-school students. Indeed, one of my hopes for this series is that it challenges the narrow assumption that only university faculty and graduate students are capable of making original contributions to literary scholarship. It simply isn't so. These volumes, produced in full collaboration with my students at Stanford Online High School, are proof that high-school English students belong in active scholarly conversations – not just as listeners but as speakers.

Ben Wiebracht, Series Editor
Stanford Online High School
Stanford University

Portrait of Dr. John Matthews,
George Romney, 1786. Tate.

Stipple engraving of Jane Austen, 1870,
after a portrait by Cassandra Austen.
National Portrait Gallery. Academic license.

14

BATH:

AN

ADUMBRATION

In Rhyme

BY AN OFFICER.

Qui capit, ille facit.

PRINTED IN THE YEAR
1795,
AND SOLD BY ALL THE BOOKSELLERS IN
BATH, BRISTOL, &c. &c.

(PRICE ONE SHILLING)

INTRODUCTION

BIOGRAPHICAL ESSAY:
JOHN MATTHEWS (1755–1826)

"Bath: An Adumbration in Rhyme" is an anonymous poem, its title page merely noting that it is "by an Officer." The *English Short Title Catalog*, however, has attributed it to the Herefordshire poet John Matthews. There are at least two reasons to question that attribution: Matthews was not in fact an officer in 1795,[1] when the poem was published, and an earlier bibliography, the *Bibliotheca Somersetensis* of 1902, attributes the poem to one John *Morgan* Matthews.[2] But neither of these objections is fatal. Matthews had adopted fictional personae in other works, and there is no evidence to support the existence of a poet named "John Morgan Matthews" in the 1790s; the middle name in the *Bibliotheca* was likely an error. Meanwhile, similarities in style and diction between the "Adumbration" and Matthews' other poems make his authorship plausible. For these reasons, we have decided to follow the *ESTC* in attributing the poem to Matthews.

John Matthews was born at Burton Court, a handsome country house near the village of Linton in Herefordshire, about a hundred miles from Jane Austen's childhood home of Steventon. Like Austen, Matthews was a member of the rural gentry, that top five percent of

---

[1] Henry Connor (medical historian, University of Birmingham), email message to Wiebracht, February 14, 2021.
[2] Green, *Bibliotheca Somersetensis*, vol. 1, 381.

the population which enjoyed such an outsized share of the nation's property and political representation. Unlike Austen, he was an only child set to inherit considerable wealth, which meant that his financial prospects were much more secure. He received a traditional gentleman's education, spending two years at Eton and then matriculating at Oxford, where he earned a BA (1778) and an MA (1779).[1] His studies up to that point would have focused on Greek and Roman authors, and indeed, Matthews' poetry shows him to have been an able classicist.

Matthews then embarked on a brief but remarkably successful medical career, one that saw him earn a Bachelor of Medicine, a medical doctorate, an appointment at St. George's Hospital, and a fellowship at the Royal College of Physicians in just two years.[2] The high point of Matthews' medical career came in 1784, when he was chosen to deliver the College's annual Goulstonian Lectures. For three days, he addressed some of the most distinguished physicians in England, perhaps performing a live dissection of a cadaver in the process, as was stipulated in the original bequest that funded the lectureship.[3]

A few months before Matthews read those lectures, however, an event had occurred that turned his life in a new direction. In late April of 1784, an elderly spinster named Elizabeth Skinner died, leaving the majority of her £80,000 fortune to Matthews.[4] It was a prodigious windfall, on the order of £10M ($14M) in today's money, according to the retail price index. Matthews was a prosperous man before the bequest: he had married an heiress, Elizabeth Ellis (1757–1823), and his medical career was flourishing. But with his new fortune, paid work of any kind was unnecessary, and Matthews accordingly retired to Herefordshire at the ripe old age of twenty nine.[5] Matthews' life as a

---

[1] Connor, "John Matthews," 98.

[2] Ibid., 98.

[3] Farrell, "RCP lectureships."

[4] "News," *Whitehall Evening Post*, May 1, 1784. Matthews and his wife named their next son Charles Skinner out of apparent gratitude to this benefactress. It is not known precisely how Mrs. Skinner was connected to the family, though she did hail from the same parish, Much Marcle, as Matthews' wife Elizabeth.

[5] In doing so, Matthews was following a common life path for physicians from wealthy families. For such men, a medical career was a respectable, temporary source of income that could be given up as soon as they inherited the family property (Lane, "Medical Practitioners," 358). Matthews, though, received his property earlier than most, and from an unconventional quarter.

practicing physician was over. His life as a country gentleman had begun.

Matthews' social ascent reached an important threshold in 1788 when he purchased an estate near the city of Hereford and built a splendid manor house on it, which he named Belmont.[1] He spared little expense in improving this property, hiring Humphry Repton (1752–1818), one of the most prominent landscape designers of the day, to lay out extensive gardens and parks.[2] But Matthews cared about utility as well as beauty. Records indicate that he took an active interest in practical matters like agriculture and animal husbandry, a sign that he wished to improve the lives of the small farmers who rented his land.[3] In this happy combination of qualities, Matthews is not far from Austen's ideal of the landlord. Men like Mr. Darcy and Mr. Knightley combine a healthy pride in the beauty of their properties with a pragmatic concern for their dependents. Darcy in particular has taken great care to preserve and improve his grounds at Pemberley, without neglecting the regular people who live on his land. Even his arch-enemy, Mr. Wickham, has to concede that he is known to be "liberal and generous, […] to assist his tenants, and relieve the poor."[4]

Matthews was capable of looking beyond his immediate property as well. He helped to fund and manage numerous charities, and was extensively involved in the internal affairs of his county. Despite having no military experience, Matthews founded and commanded a Herefordshire volunteer corps in 1798 to contribute to the country's defense in the event of a French invasion (thereafter he preferred to be called Col. Matthews).[5] Austen herself was familiar with the volunteers. Her brother Edward Austen Knight (1767–1852), also a prosperous landowner, founded and captained the Godmersham & Molash Company of East Kent Volunteers.[6] None of the volunteer corps ever saw action, but they did lift public morale. They helped create a sense of national unity, and, because membership was voluntary, they served as a symbol of British liberty and a foil to the French military, which relied on mass conscription.[7]

---

[1] Courtney and Nutt, "Matthews, John."
[2] Whitehead, *Historic Parks*, 18.
[3] Connor, "John Matthews," 102.
[4] Austen, *Pride and Prejudice*, 59.
[5] Connor, "John Matthews," 102.
[6] Le Faye, *Jane Austen*, 140.
[7] Gee, *British Volunteer Movement*, 10.

Though Matthews does not appear to have been politically ambitious, he was willing to serve in public office when called upon. He became mayor of Hereford in 1793 upon the death of the incumbent, and in 1803 he stepped in to represent Herefordshire in the House of Commons after all the candidates for the seat were disqualified for "treating" (bribing voters with refreshments).[1] Though not a frequent participant in Parliamentary debates, he could be vocal when the issue touched directly on his experience.[2] As Colonel of the First Regiment of Herefordshire Local Militia, he spoke fervently in defense of the existing volunteer system and against mandatory military training. And as a former doctor, he lent his support to Edward Jenner's (1749–1823) smallpox vaccine, a vast improvement over earlier methods of inoculation.

Where did poetry figure into the life of this energetic and public-spirited man? In literature as in politics, Matthews does not seem to have craved fame: he published anonymously and infrequently, and did not object when his most successful poem, *Eloisa en Dishabille* (1780), was attributed to another writer (perhaps because that piece, written during his university days, was rather salacious). In most of his work, the tone is boisterous and satirical, and the themes decidedly earthy. He is the only known poet in English, for instance, to write an "Ode to Cloacina" (1782), the Roman goddess of sewers. Matthews' trademark as a stylist, meanwhile, is his delight in polysyllabic rhymes, some of them outrageously tortured: "glue t' ye"/"beauty" is perhaps his worst.[3] All in all, poetry seems to have provided Matthews with occasional relief from his regular duties and an outlet for a mischievous sense of humor; it was never a vocation. Still, a subtle pride in his literary talent does occasionally peek through in the surviving materials on Matthews. A painting he commissioned in 1786 from the artist George Romney (1734–1802) shows him in a poet's pose, holding a slender volume.[4] Those who knew him, too, saw his poetry as an important part of his life. His obituary, possibly written by a family member, dwells at some length on "the peculiar grace and felicity" of

---

[1] Connor, "John Matthews," 100-102.

[2] Williams and Thorne, "Matthews, John."

[3] Matthews, *Eloisa en Dishabille*, 20.

[4] Romney, *Dr. John Matthews* (see p. vi in this volume). Dr. Connor informs us that the volume in the painting also presents Matthews as a physician with a liberal education, rather than a surgeon or apothecary, who would have received only practical training (email message to Wiebracht, April 6, 2021).

his "poetical effusions."[1]

The Oxford Dictionary of National Biography, taking a dimmer view of Matthews' work, tells us that much of his poetry was "badly received" and that some of it was regarded by contemporaries as "contemptible."[2] That assessment needs revision. For one, the only contemporary who used the term "contemptible" was Richard Payne Knight (1751–1824), the target of one of Matthews' satires and therefore hardly the most objective critic.[3] In fact, most reviews of Matthews' work were positive.[4] But the claim that Matthews' poetry is bad also misses the point: its occasional badness (or pretense of such) is part of its humor. In a short poem called "To the Critics," part of Matthews' only book-length collection of poems, he imagines a dialogue between himself and a reader who can barely endure his forced rhymes and "slovenly" meter. He tries to placate this exacting critic with several attempts at an elevated style, but without success, and decides in the end to proceed in his "own style and manner."[5] It would be simplistic to read such a poem as evidence that actual critics disapproved of Matthews' work. In this case, the reproachful critic is a comic device, not unlike the Host of the *Canterbury Tales*, who tells Chaucer that his "Tale of Sir Thopas" is "nat worth a tord."[6] An actual critic for the *Quarterly Review*, on the contrary, considered "To the Critics" "[one] of the prettiest things in his book."[7]

The persona of the cheerful "literary scrub," as Matthews once described himself, was the one in which he seems to have been most comfortable.[8] The main joke of "An Ode to Cloacina" (1782) is that bad poetry, like his own, is going to end up as toilet paper. While other poets had alluded to this grim destiny, none embraced it as enthusiastically as Matthews. He actually had the poem printed on especially soft paper for the better comfort of his readers, and offered to make special editions on silver paper for the use of fine lords and ladies. One appreciative reviewer, getting in on the joke, suggested as

---

[1] *Hereford Journal*, January 18, 1826, 3.
[2] Courtney and Nutt, "Matthews, John."
[3] Knight, *The Landscape*, ix.
[4] We provide a list of reviews of Matthews' poetry at the end of the bibliography. The tone of them ranges from mildly appreciative to decidedly positive.
[5] Matthews, *Fables from La Fontaine*, 175.
[6] Chaucer, "Tale of Melibee," line 930.
[7] *Quarterly Review* 23.46 (1820), 459.
[8] Matthews, "Sketch," 20.

an epigraph "Non *posteris*, sed *posterioribus*": not for posterity, but for posteriors.[1] Those who read Matthews in his own playful spirit seem to have enjoyed his self-deprecating vulgarity.

Despite his modesty, however, Matthews was capable of landing a satirical punch. His "Sketch, from *The Landscape*" (1794) mocked the new enthusiasm for "picturesque" landscapes, those that featured wilderness, ruins, and other forms of rugged and majestic "sublimity." As readers of Austen know, picturesque principles, applied too strictly, could lead to some absurd conclusions. In *Northanger Abbey* (1817), the ironic narrator tells us that "Catherine was so hopeful a scholar [of the picturesque], that when they gained the top of Beechen Cliff, she voluntarily rejected the whole city of Bath, as unworthy to make part of a landscape."[2] Matthews' strategy is similar: he exposes the excesses of picturesque theory by pretending to defend it. At one point, he rails against smooth, open parks (like his own), suggesting that some bare yew trees and wild hedges would enliven the scene, "[j]ust as rich warts, and rubied pimples, / Are far more picturesque than dimples."[3] One reviewer praised the poem as a good specimen of Horatian satire, the kind that criticizes in a genial spirit.[4] But perhaps a better tribute to the poem's efficacy came in the angry response of its immediate target, the scholar Richard Payne Knight, who felt the need to add a preface to the second edition of his own poem, *The Landscape* (1794), refuting the charges of this "doggerel ode."[5]

At some point in the 1810's, Matthews entered what he called a "painful and long protracted indisposition."[6] To while away the gloomy hours, he embarked on the most ambitious literary project of his life, which he published in 1820 as *Fables from La Fontaine, in English Verse*. Despite the title, the collection was not really a translation of the great French fabulist Jean de la Fontaine (1621–1695). Most of the poems in the collection are original and highly contemporary pieces only loosely based on his predecessor's simple moral tales. It is here that we get the clearest picture of Matthews' political and religious views. The fables show him to be a firm supporter of the Anglican establishment and a believer in British exceptionalism. Most of all, they

---

[1] *Critical Review* 53 (1782), 233.
[2] Austen, *Northanger Abbey*, 77.
[3] Matthews, "Sketch," 11.
[4] *English Review* 24 (1794), 471.
[5] Knight, *Landscape*, ix.
[6] Matthews, *Fables from la Fontaine*, viii.

reveal that Matthews was "decidedly hostile to levelling," or the elimination of class distinctions through democratic reform.[1] Take the familiar tale of "The Dog and his Reflection" (which la Fontaine inherited from Aesop). A dog, carrying home a bone, sees his reflection while crossing a bridge and mistakes it for another dog, carrying an even juicier bone. He tries to snatch this new prize and loses his actual bone in the process. In Matthews' hands, this general warning against greed and jealousy takes on a political meaning: it serves to illustrate the folly of the French revolutionaries (the "brain-sick Demogogues of France"), who lost the attainable benefit of a limited monarchy in their pursuit of an illusory democratic ideal.[2] In 1820, such anti-democratic views would have been firmly in the English mainstream. After witnessing the carnage of the French Revolution, whose aftermath plunged Europe into more than two decades of ruinous war, many British people were skeptical of radical social change and convinced that stability was best ensured by a clear-cut social hierarchy and a healthy deference toward existing institutions – the bone in the mouth rather than the bone in the water.

Like Matthews, Austen was no supporter of wholesale levelling. Social climbers like Lucy Steele from *Sense and Sensibility* (1811) and Isabella Thorpe from *Northanger Abbey* are generally frowned upon in her work. Even amiable members of the lower orders are discouraged from climbing the ladder. The low-born Harriet Smith from *Emma* (1816), sweet and pretty though she may be, is not a suitable match for a gentleman, and Emma's pursuit of such a match for her friend is her most persistent folly in the novel. At the same time, while Austen did have a basic respect for the social hierarchy, she tended to interpret its boundaries generously. Her novels are full of characters like Mrs. Jennings or Mr. Bingley who have bought their way into the landed gentry, and Austen does not judge them harshly for it. On the contrary, her most stringent satire is reserved for the over-rigid enforcers of class distinctions, characters like Lady Catherine de Bourgh who insist upon the respect due to their social position, but neglect or misinterpret the moral responsibilities that accompany it. In short, Matthews and Austen shared a conservative commitment to the structures of deference and patronage that organized rural life. But while Matthews saw the main threat to that order as coming from the outside, in the

---

[1] Ibid., vii.
[2] Ibid., 253.

form of democratic (and French) political ideas, Austen saw the main threat as internal, in the moral failings of the gentry itself.

John Matthews' final years were marred by poor health and financial woes. He never recovered from the illness he refers to in *Fables from La Fontaine*, which his obituary described as a "protracted malady of intense suffering."[1] In 1825, a bank he had founded, and on which he depended for much of his income, collapsed, one of many such casualties during the so-called Panic of 1825.[2] He died the following year and his beloved Belmont had to be sold. Much of Matthews' landscaping was destroyed when the property was converted to a golf course in the twentieth century. His poetry, too, quickly fell out of print, and since then it has been known only to specialists. That last misfortune, at least, can be remedied. We hope this book plays a small part in restoring to the notice of modern readers the work of this genial, witty contemporary of Jane Austen.

---

[1] *Hereford Journal*, January 18, 1826, 3.
[2] Connor, "John Matthews," 102.

CONTEXTUAL ESSAY: THE BATH SATIRE

The poem contained in this volume, "Bath: An Adumbration in Rhyme," is a humorous picture of a typical day in the most fashionable resort town of late Georgian England. During the Bath season from October to June, high society would flock to the city. For the gouty and the infirm, Bath offered relief: its mineral waters, whether bathed in or drunk, were thought to relieve a variety of complaints. For everyone else, there was endless entertainment. As Matthews puts it, "There the circle of day is one scene of delight, / From morning to noon, from noon until night" (lines 5-6).[1] In the morning, visitors repaired to the Pump Room to drink the waters and meet with friends. The afternoon was high time for shopping, strolling, and riding. Bath itself, with its many parks and its stunning neoclassical architecture, afforded pleasant walks; and for more enterprising visitors, there were scenic views to be had from nearby Beechen Cliff and Lansdown Hill. It was in the evening, however, that Bath donned its brightest colors. There were plays, operas, and concerts. There were fireworks and other outdoor displays. And, at least four times a week, there were the public balls for which Bath was famous. At these gatherings, open to all visitors for a modest subscription, guests would dance, eat, play cards, and just maybe fall in love.

Bath was also the city that Jane Austen knew best. She first visited the city in 1797 and lived there from 1801–1806 after her father gave up his living as rector of Steventon. This familiarity shows in her novels. Every one of them at least refers to Bath, and large portions of *Northanger Abbey* and *Persuasion* (1817) are set there. According to some, Austen's own feelings about Bath soured after she moved there,[2] but

---

[1] When quoting "Bath: An Adumbration in Rhyme," we cite the text of the poem as it appears in this volume; for our editorial principles, see pp. 28-29.

[2] There is little doubt that Austen was sorry to leave Steventon Rectory for Bath: according to family lore, she fainted upon hearing the news of the move. It is true

there is no doubt that the city provided lasting fuel for her literary imagination.

Matthews' "Adumbration" (the word means a sketch or outline) is a valuable resource for readers of Jane Austen for two reasons. First, it captures the city just two years before Austen experienced it for the first time. Such contemporaneity matters. Austen herself worried that the portrait of Bath offered in *Northanger Abbey*, based largely on her 1797 visit, was out-of-date in 1816, as the novel was finally being prepared for publication.[1] In pairing Matthews and Austen, there is no such mismatch. The sights, sounds and people he describes were the very ones that would have greeted a twenty-one-year-old Austen or a seventeen-year-old Catherine Morland. Indeed, when we read Matthews alongside Austen, new shades of meaning emerge in her work. To take an example, one morning Isabella Thorpe, Catherine's superficial and coquettish friend, describes a hat she "longed for" in a shop on Milsom Street.[2] Could this have taken place at the hat shop of Elizabeth Mandell, located on Milsom Street and mentioned in Matthews' poem as a destination for flashy young men hoping to catch the attention of female shoppers?[3] If so, perhaps Isabella was on the hunt for men and not just millinery that particular morning.

In addition to giving us a street-level view of Austen's Bath, Matthews' poem helps us appreciate the larger literary context of Austen's Bath novels. His "Adumbration" belongs to a genre of poetry that, while little read today, was highly popular in the late eighteenth century and no doubt familiar to Austen: namely, satires of Bath. This tradition originated in 1766 with the publication of Christopher Anstey's (1724–1805) *New Bath Guide*. Comprised of a series of fictional letters, the *New Bath Guide* follows the adventures of a gullible party of visitors to the city. These tourists, members of the Blunderhead family, embrace the delights of Bath wholeheartedly,

---

as well that her late Bath novel, *Persuasion*, is much more critical of Bath than her early one, *Northanger Abbey*, mainly written before her residence in the city. Nevertheless, it is hard to imagine that Austen ever became completely cynical toward Bath. As Maggie Lane writes, "Bath existed for pleasure, and it needed someone much more sour-tempered or narrowminded not to derive pleasure from it" (*Jane Austen's World*, 34).

[1] See Austen's "Advertisement" to the first edition of *Northanger Abbey*.

[2] Austen, *Northanger Abbey*, 24.

[3] Historian Trevor Fawcett was the first to notice this possible connection. See *Bath Commercialis'd*, 53-54.

shelling out money for expensive clothes, attending balls, and sampling the waters in the Pump Room. Eventually, though, they learn the hard way that Bath isn't quite the paradise it seems. The dashing captain proves to be a scoundrel. The beauties who dazzle in the evening look "paler than Ashes" the next morning, without the benefit of cosmetics.[1] Even the fabled waters of Bath have a dark side. Anstey implies that the curative beverage quaffed in the Pump Room is drawn directly from the baths below, so that "while little Tabby was washing her Rump, / The Ladies kept drinking it out of the Pump" (42).

The New Bath Guide, one of the bestsellers of the late 18th century, inspired numerous imitators, who largely followed Anstey in style and content. Three characteristics define this body of poetry. The first is an emphasis on false display. In the satirical tradition, Bath and its visitors are always trying to appear better than they are: richer, more beautiful, more dignified. The second characteristic is the use of anapestic couplets, which Anstey helped re-introduce to English poetry after a period of neglect. Anapestic meter, which has a relatively high proportion of unstressed syllables, reads quickly and is well suited to comic content; limericks, for example, are usually anapestic. The third, in part a result of the meter, is a breezy, cheerful tone – a marked departure from the moral fury of much early-eighteenth-century satire.[2] The reader is invited to laugh at Bath, not to judge it. Perhaps there is even an implied invitation to go and see for yourself. As Shaun Regan writes, this genre "maintained a fine balance between popular advertisement and satiric critique."[3] Anstey's original satire was certainly taken as friendly ribbing by most readers. Indeed, the high society of Bath welcomed Anstey when he moved there in 1770, and he enjoyed harmonious relationships with his neighbors, high and low alike, for over forty years. Bath and the Bath satire were generally on good terms.

Matthews' "Adumbration" fits squarely in this tradition. His critiques of Bath are, for the most part, the same ones that Anstey had launched thirty years before. The men are foppish, the ladies pretentious, the waters contaminated. Sometimes, Matthews' reliance

---

[1] Anstey, *New Bath Guide*, 85. Hereafter cited parenthetically by page number.
[2] In the *New Bath Guide*, this cheerful tone is partly due to Anstey's primary narrator, Simkin Blunderhead, whose naiveté leads to a positive outlook on the city's events and inhabitants. Later Bath satirists, who often used more jaded narrators, were never quite able to match Anstey in this regard.
[3] Regan, "Bathing in Verse," 138.

on Anstey is close indeed, as in the following lines:

> [*Anstey*]
> They say it is right that for every Glass
> A Tune you should take, that the Waters may pass. (42)

> [*Matthews*]
> For the doctors all say, the waters to pass,
> You should hear a brisk tune between ev'ry glass. (lines 11-12)

It is not an isolated instance. Echoes of Anstey can be found throughout the poem: even Matthews' opening line – "Of all the gay cities in Britain renowned" (line 1) – mimics Anstey's "Of all the gay Places the World can afford" (43).

Matthews does break some new ground, too. At times, anticipating Austen, he finds humor in small, private moments ignored by most other Bath satirists. One such moment occurs just after breakfast, when the visitor to the city settles down to read the newspaper – but not for news. The Bath papers printed the names of all the recent arrivals in order of prestige, so the visitor's first priority is to ascertain "where [his] own name appears in the list"; this is the "politics" that most concerns him (lines 23, 29). These sorts of light satirical touches shift the focus from the broad caricatures which were the staple of Bath satire to the minor vanities of everyday life in the city.

Matthews also follows Anstey and the majority of the Bath satirists in employing anapestic couplets, a form he knew well. His popular 1780 parody of Pope, *Eloisa en Dishabille*, which one poet compared favorably to Anstey's *New Bath Guide*,[1] converted Pope's stately heroic couplets into rollicking anapestic ones, and the change in the sound of the verse is half the poem's humor. A comparison of the opening lines is sufficient to show the difference.

> [*Pope, in couplets of iambic pentameter*]
> In these deep solitudes and awful cells,
> Where heav'nly pensive contemplation dwells,
> And ever-musing melancholy reigns;
> What means this tumult in a vestal's veins?[2]

---

[1] Dyer, *Poems*, 325.
[2] Pope, *Eloisa to Abelard*, 3.

[*Matthews, in couplets of anapestic tetrameter*]
Immur'd in this prison, so dull and so moping,
Where vows and high walls bar all hopes of eloping,
Where close grated windows scarce shew us the sun,
What means this strange itch in the flesh of a Nun?[1]

In the "Adumbration," Matthews' couplets are often structured to create a sense of bathos or anticlimax. In the following couplet, notice how an elegant stroll around the Pump Room turns into a bit of naughty peeping as the guests upstairs gawk at the bathers below.

So the beaux in their boots, the belles in their slippers,
Come to walk up and down, and peep at the dippers.
(lines 13-14)

The joke is not particularly sophisticated, but the delivery is effective: raise an expectation in the first line (here, for polite romance), subvert it in the second. In this case, a well-timed hitch in the meter makes the punchline all the more jarring: "and peep at the dippers" begins with an iamb rather than an anapest, disrupting not just our standard picture of beaux and belles, but the pace of the line as well. Such tricks of the trade show Matthews to have been an able prosodist.

Finally, Matthews largely preserves the genial tone of Anstey's original. The city he sketches may be vain and ridiculous, but it is nevertheless full of energy. Consider his description of youthful flirtation at a public ball. A more sour-tempered poet might have griped about low-cut dresses and rouge, but Matthews prefers to be indulgent. For him, the dance floor is a place where

[…] each lovesick nymph, may hear her dear swain,
In whispering murmurs, declare his sweet pain,
Where the sigh, and the smile, and the soft gentle squeeze,
All contribute the hearts of each other to ease;
Where no prudish aunts, through old maidenly spite,
Can hinder these symptoms of youthful delight. (lines 117-122)

---

[1] Matthews, *Eloisa*, 9.

Of course, the reality falls somewhat short of the diction; these young people are not heroically in love, as phrases like "love-sick nymph" and "sweet pain" would suggest. They are simply having a good time. Still, the scene is a pleasant one, perhaps all the more so for being closer to real life. Bath might not always live up to its billing as the center of elegant amusement, but it remains, in Matthews' poem, decidedly fun.

If Matthews' satire is generally mild, at some points it can strike modern readers as rather cruel. He takes several shots, for example, at older, unmarried women visiting Bath. We see a glimpse of this in Matthews' joke about the "old maidenly spite" of the chaperones at the public ball, jealous of their charges' happiness. Elsewhere, he is more expansive:

> Let's haste to the Crescent, that gay promenade,
> Where many appointments and parties are made,
> Where fusty old maidens, to look like the Graces,
> With well-padded bellies and well-painted faces,
> With many an ogle, a simper and smile,
> Attempt the soft heart of some swain to beguile. (lines 55-60)

Such jibing is a credit neither to Matthews' generosity nor to his creativity, but it is representative of the larger satirical tradition. Old maids or "spinsters" were routinely mocked by Bath satirists. These visitors came to Bath, like everyone else, for a variety of reasons – to take the waters, to meet friends, to shop, to dance. In the satires, though, one overriding motive compels them: husband-hunting. The stereotypical Bath spinster was a scrawny, unattractive woman (thus the need for the "fusty old maidens" to pad their bellies) whose romantic disappointments had made her either perpetually bitter, desperately flirtatious, or both.[1] Of course, underlying the stereotype

---

[1] The gaunt and graceless Tabitha Bramble from Tobias Smollett's (1721–1771) *The Expedition of Humphry Clinker* (1771) is perhaps the fullest realization of the type.

> Mrs. Tabitha Bramble is a maiden of forty-five. In her person, she is tall, raw-boned, aukward, flat-chested, and stooping; her complexion is sallow and freckled; […] her nose long, sharp […]; and her long neck shriveled into a thousand wrinkles – In her temper, she is proud, stiff, vain, imperious, prying, malicious, greedy, and uncharitable. In all likelihood, her natural austerity has been soured by disappointment in love; for her

was the old assumption that the value of women consisted primarily in their ability to attract men and bear children. It was sometimes difficult for the period to imagine that an older, unmarried woman might have sources of meaning and enjoyment separate from wifedom and motherhood: thus she must always be brooding over her failure to marry or scheming how to reverse it. Even the shriveled body of the spinster is a testament to this assumption (widows, by contrast, were usually depicted as plump). Apart from child-bearing, the female body was thought to have little purpose, and so, in spinsterhood, it withered away. In Bath, such misogyny was amplified for the simple reason that spinsters were more visible there than elsewhere. They frequented the baths and public amusements, dressed up, and generally tried to have a good time. Confronted with the spectacle of spinsters enjoying themselves, the Bath satire usually responded with one-dimensional ridicule, and Matthews, who captures much of the fun and ease of the genre, captures this element of it as well.

The satirical tradition that Matthews exemplifies would have been familiar to Jane Austen, a voracious reader and a visitor to the city herself (and later, a resident). In some respects, Austen is a participant in that tradition, particularly in *Northanger Abbey*. Like Anstey's *New Bath Guide*, *Northanger Abbey* is the story of a naïve visitor from the country who is at first dazzled by the city, but ultimately comes to see it in a more sober light. Along the way she meets a variety of Bath types: the swaggering beau (John Thorpe), the insincere coquette (his sister Isabella), and the rakish officer (Captain Tilney), to name a few. A parallel subplot runs through Austen and Anstey as well: both Isabella Thorpe and Anstey's Jenny flirt with handsome captains who jilt them in the end. As in all Bath satires, the pleasures of Bath never quite live up to their billing. The guests at Catherine's first ball resemble a "mob" more than a polite assembly, and while she gamely describes the evening as "[v]ery agreeable indeed," the "great yawn" she gives at the same time seems like the more honest statement.[1]

But for all Austen's mockery of the town, the novel as a whole, like

---

long celibacy is by no means owing to her dislike of matrimony: on the contrary, she has left no stone unturned to avoid the reproachful epithet of old maid. (60)

[1] Austen, *Northanger Abbey*, 11, 13.

Anstey's and Matthews' poems, does not seem harshly disposed toward it. After she has made a few friends, Catherine does enjoy the shopping, the walks, the plays and the dancing. Most of all, she enjoys the company of Henry Tilney, a charming young man she meets at one of the public balls. When she and Henry ultimately marry, they have Bath to thank for it. The Master of Ceremonies, an important Bath official, is the one to introduce them, and the leisurely, permissive culture of the city is what allows them to dance and converse so frequently and with so few strictures. For Catherine, Bath, despite its follies and vanities, does have a bit of magic after all.

Still, if Austen's Bath novels follow the satirical tradition in some respects, taken as a whole they go far beyond it. The typical Bath satire relied on obvious and outrageous spectacles, the humor of which could be seized in a moment. Austen's satire is more complicated and gradual; even if she begins with a standard type, she almost never ends there.

Take the figure of the macaroni – the hyper-fashionable man whose attempts at elegance make him ridiculous rather than impressive. Ever since Anstey, the joke was that young men in Bath were a bunch of preening, overdressed fops. According to Matthews, "the gay macaronies" (line 33) of Bath like to swagger around in boots and spurs, but you would have a hard time catching them on horseback. They prefer to "[b]estride Mandell's counter, instead of their ponies" (line 34). That is, they would rather hang around a milliner's shop flirting with the shoppers than do something vigorous and manly like go for a ride. That is how it was done before Austen: if you wanted to have a joke about the state of masculinity in Bath, you pointed to the extravagant dress and the effeminate behavior of the young men. Indeed, one satirist refused to treat a macaroni as a man at all, preferring the pronoun "it."[1]

When Austen takes up the macaroni, she does so with larger aims. Sir Walter Elliot from *Persuasion*, obsessed with his personal appearance despite his advanced years, is a middle-aged twist on the type. But Austen is not content merely to laugh at Sir Walter's narcissistic mirror-gazing. She uses it instead to launch a critique of the self-absorbed snobbery of an entire class. Sir Walter, a baronet from an old landed family, has squandered much of his fortune. To make ends meet, he decides to move the family to Bath and, in the meantime,

---

[1] Pasquin, *Postscript*, 62-63.

rent out his country seat, Kellynch Hall.[1] The tenant he finds is Admiral Croft, a rising man who has made his fortune capturing French vessels during the Napoleonic Wars. The larger reality is this: a new elite class based on merit and patriotism (Admiral Croft) is moving into the social position (Kellynch Hall) previously occupied by an old elite class (Sir Walter) which is at risk of sacrificing its claim through idleness and complacency. Sir Walter, though, is incapable of recognizing this. He seems to think Admiral Croft is a "very lucky man" to live at Kellynch Hall, and that he himself is being rather magnanimous in allowing him to do so (even though, without a tenant, he would likely have to sell the place).[2] The Bath macaroni is still recognizable; Sir Walter continues to take an absurd pride in his dress and his looks after moving to the town. But now this vanity is symbolic of a class-wide blindness, a failure to realize that the externalities of social status – titles, pedigrees, fine clothing – count for very little, may even become ridiculous, when the moral core is missing. For Matthews, the macaroni was a man in spurs who barely knew how to ride. For Austen, he was much more: an entire social class, loaded with privilege but ignorant of how to lead.

Austen's class conscience did not just manifest in criticism of the elite; it also expressed itself in sympathy for the marginalized. In this respect, she did not merely build on the satirical tradition; she directly contradicted it.

For decades before Austen visited the city, Bath had been a place where the classes collided. Partly this was by design. Beau Nash (1674-1762), Bath's original Master of Ceremonies and the man largely responsible for its rise as a premier resort town, envisioned the city as a place where men and women could mingle irrespective of class, regulated by taste and manners alone.[3] That vision proved durable. As the *New Bath Guide* of 1796 (an actual guide to the city, not to be confused with Anstey's poem) boasted, "Ceremony beyond the essential rules of politeness is totally exploded; everyone mixes in the Rooms upon an equality."[4] But of course, this liberality had limits. By

---

[1] In creating Sir Walter, Austen may have drawn inspiration from Anstey's "Liberality: Or, The Decayed Macaroni" (1788), which also features a washed-up man-of-fashion who retires to Bath out of financial necessity. We thank Shaun Regan for bringing this poem to our attention.

[2] Austen, *Persuasion*, 12.

[3] Davis and Bonsall, *History of Bath*, 121.

[4] *New Bath Guide; or, Useful Pocket Companion*, 26.

"everyone," promoters of Bath meant the aristocracy, the gentry, and people connected to the gentlemanly professions (the clergy, the military, and the law). In reality, the class system of Bath was wider and more complicated than that. Bath historians Graham Davis and Penny Bonsall write that "as the city grew in size and prestige, the social composition of its visitors broadened to include many modest clients from the middling gentry and the rising professional and commercial middle classes."[1] These new visitors strained the limits of Bath's easygoing hospitality. Some elite visitors responded by withdrawing: General Tilney, contemptuous of the company at Bath and eager to leave, is such a one. Others still came to Bath for the waters, but avoided the public assemblies in favor of private parties, whose guest lists could be more carefully curated.[2]

Bath satirists before Austen noticed this emerging dynamic and usually blamed it on the vulgarity and sheer abundance of the new visitors. The standard device was to depict an overcrowded, public space – the Pump Room, perhaps, or one of the Assembly Rooms – in which members of the lower orders stepped on the toes, knocked over the hats, and offended the nostrils of their betters. Here is Matthews' take on this convention:

> The minuets o'er, see the crowd how it presses,
> What havoc is made on the ladies' fine dresses!
> Distinction of rank in a moment is gone,
> And all eager for tea in one mass now move on;
> E'en the peeresses' selves, for whom benches were kept,
> Angry with the torrent, impetuous are swept;
> And Mistress O'Darby, the dealer in butter,
> Now sweats by the side of the sweet Lady Flutter,
> Who would certainly faint, but her senses so nice
> Are supported by smelling fat Alderman Spice,
> Whilst his Worship's white wig almost smothers the face
> Of her dainty young cousin, the dear Lady Grace.
> The Countess of Pharo is forced to huddle
> Between Doctor Squirt and his niece, Miss Di-Puddle;
> Sir Stephen Newmarket, Sir Simon Profuse,
> The Ladies St. Larum, and old Madam Goose;

---

[1] Davis and Bonsall, *History of Bath*, 114.
[2] Lane, *Jane Austen's World*, 74.

For Commoners now, so saucy are grown,
That Cabbage the tailor, Lady Tombstone,
The Duchess of Basset, and Marquis de Frieze
All bundle together in one loving squeeze. (lines 83-102)

The rather blunt message here is that "distinction of rank" is necessary for social order, and that if the classes mingle, chaos will ensue. Of course, Matthews is mining the spectacle mainly for humor, but that only shows how ingrained class prejudices could be. Matthews does not need to explain to his readers why it is a problem for a butter dealer and a lady to attend the same evening amusement. He simply jams the two together in a tight space, and trusts (probably with good reason) that the reader's sense of the absurd will automatically be tickled.

Austen's take on the social mixture of Bath is quite a bit more sophisticated and, indeed, sympathetic. Unlike earlier Bath satirists, she never treats the mingling of the classes as ridiculous on its face. Isabella Thorpe may over-reach in her bid for Captain Tilney, but this violation of class boundaries is obvious neither to Catherine nor to her brother, and even the perceptive Henry has trouble explaining to her why the match is unlikely. Indeed, in the case of Isabella and Captain Tilney, class is only one factor at play. Isabella's beauty, moral looseness, and lack of male guardianship all combine to explain why Captain Tilney is eager to woo but unwilling to marry her.

Catherine's marriage to Henry also tests the flexibility of the class system. Henry's family is far wealthier than Catherine's, but on the other hand, he is a clergyman and she a clergyman's daughter; in that respect they seem well suited. In a marginal case like this, a novelist has the power to shape her readers' understanding of where the boundaries lie. She does this not by deciding whether to allow the lovers to marry: in a comedy, marriage is a foregone conclusion. Instead, she teaches her readers what the norms are by dramatizing the reaction of society to the marriage. Are friends and family opposed? Is society scandalized? In *Northanger Abbey*, neither is the case, with one exception: General Tilney. When Catherine and Henry wed, "every body smile[s]," and the General, the would-be upholder of class divisions, is written off as a greedy curmudgeon, out of step with the wider community.[1] The lesson for the reader in all this is more

---

[1] Austen, *Northanger Abbey*, 174.

progressive than it seems. Had Henry and Catherine married in defiance of society, the message would be that marriages involving a disparity of wealth are exceptional, reserved for the courageous and the deeply-in-love. As it is, the message is that such unions are typical, and that a young woman need not be a heroine to claim her right to one.

In her later Bath novel, *Persuasion*, Austen shows an even finer sensitivity to the nuances of the Bath class system. In Matthews' passage, the very name of a character tells you where they fit on the social ladder: "Cabbage the tailor," for example. No such easy determination is possible with Mrs. Smith, the widowed invalid whom Anne Elliot visits in Bath. As Sir Walter complains, a Smith could be anyone. As a young woman, Mrs. Smith married a wealthy man, but he wasted his money and she was left almost destitute upon his death. Afflicted by ill health as well, she moved to Bath in the hopes of treatment. When Anne visits her old friend, she finds her leading a marginal existence, living in tiny lodgings and venturing out only for doctor-prescribed bathing. It is easy enough for the rest of Bath society to write her off. Sir Walter certainly does, even though, as a downwardly mobile exile to Bath, he has more in common with Mrs. Smith than he might like to admit. Historically, too, women like Mrs. Smith were generally treated with scorn, if they were noticed at all. As we have seen, Bath satirists before Austen almost always mocked the city's high population of unmarried women, and the Bath newspapers usually put them at the bottom of their lists of arrivals.

Defying her father, literary precedent, and the culture of Bath alike, Anne sticks by her old schoolmate. She understands the painfulness of Mrs. Smith's situation. She hasn't just lost a husband or suffered a financial blow. She has fallen through one of the cracks in the English class system, and now has no place in it. Despite her birth and education, she is no longer welcome in the polite society of Bath; because of them, she has no place among the mercantile and laboring classes. As a woman, she cannot repair her fortunes with a new career, and as a woman who has lost her beauty and health, she cannot hope to remarry. It is a credit to Austen's social insight that she is able to express the plight of a character like Mrs. Smith, and it is a credit to her generosity, a generosity not shared by most of the Bath satirists, that she could sympathize with it.

To conclude, the poem included in this volume is a good specimen of a lively, playful genre of poetry that flourished in late Georgian Bath and then faded with the heyday of the city itself. But our purpose in publishing it is not antiquarian. Instead, we contend that, because Austen matters today, so does Matthews. He gives us a picture of a typical day in Bath that, as luck would have it, is almost exactly contemporaneous with Austen's first visit to the city. Beyond that, he shows us the satirical tradition that existed before Austen, and in so doing helps us appreciate just how revolutionary her Bath novels were. Plenty of writers, including Matthews, set their satirical sights on Bath, but none, until Austen, analyzed with such clarity the tangle of social prejudices that underlay the "gay city," or drew with such subtlety the hoping, scheming, struggling humans who passed through it.

BIBLIOGRAPHY

Anstey, Christopher. *The New Bath Guide: or, Memoirs of the B-R-D Family. In a Series of Poetical Epistles.* London: J. Dodsley, 1766.

Austen, Jane. *Northanger Abbey.* New York: Norton, 2004.

Austen, Jane. *Persuasion.* New York: Norton, 1995.

Austen, Jane. *Pride and Prejudice.* New York: Norton, 2016.

Chaucer, Geoffrey. "From 'The Prologue and Tale of Melibee.'" *The Canterbury Tales.* New York: Norton, 2005.

Connor, Henry. "John Matthews (1755–1826) of Belmont." *Transactions of the Woolhope Naturalists' Field Club* 66 (2018): 98-108.

Courtney, W.P. and Claire L. Nutt. "Matthews, John (bap. 1755, d. 1826), physician and poet." *Oxford Dictionary of National Biography.* September 23, 2004. https://www.oxforddnb.com/view/10.1093/ref:odnb/97801 98614128.001.0001/odnb-9780198614128-e-18345.

Davis, Graham and Penny Bonsall. *A History of Bath: Image and Reality.* Lancaster, UK: Carnegie Publishing, 2006.

Dyer, George. *Poems.* London: Longman and Rees, 1801.

Farrell, Alana. "19th century RCP lectureships now online." *Royal College of Physicians.* Accessed March 31, 2021. https://history.rcplondon.ac.uk/blog/19th-century-rcp-lectureships-now-online.

Fawcett, Trevor. *Bath Commercialis'd: Shops, Trades and Market at the 18th-Century Spa.* Bath: RUTON, 2002.

Gee, Austin. *The British Volunteer Movement 1794-1814.* London: Clarendon, 2003.

Green, Emanuel. *Bibliotheca Somersetensis: A Catalogue of Books, Pamphlets, Single Sheets, and Broadsides in Some Way Connected with the County of Somerset.* Taunton, UK: Barnicott and Pearce, 1902.

Knight, Richard Payne. *The Landscape, a Didactic Poem.* London: W.

Bulmer, 1795.

Lane, Joan. "The Medical Practitioners of Provincial England in 1783." *Medical History* 28 (1984): 353-371.

Lane, Maggie. *Jane Austen's World: The Life and Times of England's Most Popular Author*. London: Carlton, 1996.

Le Faye, Deirdre. *Jane Austen: A Family Record*. Cambridge: Cambridge UP, 2004.

Matthews, John. *Eloisa en Dishabille*. London: Faulder, 1780.

Matthews, John. *Fables from La Fontaine*. London: John Murray, 1820.

Matthews, John. "A Sketch, from *The Landscape, a Didactic Poem*." London: Faulder, 1794.

The New Bath Guide; or, Useful Pocket Companion. Bath: R. Cruttwell, 1796.

Pasquin, Anthony [John Williams]. *A Postscript to the New Bath Guide*. London: J. Strahan, 1790.

Pope, Alexander. *Eloisa to Abelard*. Glasgow: R. and A. Foulis, 1751.

Regan, Shaun. "Bathing in Verse: Christopher Anstey's *The New Bath Guide* and Georgian Resort Satire." In *Spa Culture and Literature in England, 1500-1800*, edited by Sophie Chiari and Samuel Cuisinier-Delorme. Cham, Switzerland: Palgrave, 2021.

[Review of *Fables from la Fontaine*]. *Quarterly Review* 23.46 (1820): 455-463.

[Review of "Ode to Cloacina"]. *Critical Review* 53 (1782): 232-233.

[Review of "A Sketch, from *The Landscape, a Didactic Poem*"]. *English Review* 24 (1794): 471.

Romney, George. *Dr. John Matthews*. 1786. Oil on canvas, 146cm x 121.3cm (57.5in x 47.8in). Tate, London, England. https://www.tate.org.uk/art/artworks/romney-dr-john-matthews-n04489.

Smollett, Tobias. *The Expedition of Humphry Clinker*. Oxford: Oxford UP, 2009.

Whitehead, David. *A Survey of Historic Parks and Gardens in Herefordshire*. [Hereford]: Hereford and Worcester Gardens Trust, 2001.

Williams, M.J. and R.G. Thorne. "Matthews, John (1755–1826), of Belmont, Herefs." *The History of Parliament: the House of Commons*, ed. R.G. Thorne. 1986. https://www.historyofparliamentonline.org/volume/1790-1820/member/matthews-john-1755-1826.

CONTEMPORARY REVIEWS
OF MATTHEWS' POETRY

Eloisa en Dishabille (1780)

- Dyer, George. "The Redress." *Poems*. London: Longman and Rees, 1801. This poem is not a review *per se*, but it does praise *Eloisa en Dishabille*, comparing it favorably to Anstey's *New Bath Guide*. See p. 325.

"Ode to Cloacina" (1782)

- *Critical Review, or Annals of Literature* 53 (1782): 232-233.
- *Monthly Review or Literary Journal* 67 (1782): 387.

"A Sketch, from *The Landscape, a Didactic Poem*" (1794)

- *English Review* 24 (1794): 471.
- *Monthly Review or Literary Journal, Enlarged* 16 (1794): 318-320.

Fables from La Fontaine (1820)

- *Quarterly Review* 23.46 (1820): 455-463.

FURTHER READING

Very little has been written on John Matthews' life and work. Henry Connor's article "John Matthews (1755–1826) of Belmont" (see bibliography) is the most thorough biography available. The only substantial survey of his poetry, meanwhile, is the one offered in the introduction of this volume. Most of Matthews' other poems, listed on the opposite page, can be found on Google Books for free, though none of them is currently in print.

Readers interested in the genre of the Bath satire are especially recommended to read Christopher Anstey's 1766 poem *The New Bath Guide*, the original Bath satire and the best, at least until *Northanger Abbey*. The poem can be found on Google Books or in a recent critical edition edited by Annick Cossic (Peter Lang, 2010). Shaun Regan's recent chapter "Bathing in Verse" in *Spa Culture and Literature in England, 1500-1800* (Palgrave, 2021) offers a helpful survey of the genre of the Bath satire and makes a convincing case for its significance. Regan shows that this type of verse spread to other resort towns as well, where it played an important role in defining the ideal of sociability in the late eighteenth century.

There is currently a lively debate among Austen scholars over her relationship to Bath. Was Austen a country girl at heart who despised the cramped and busy city and its artificial pleasures? Or did she share Catherine Morland's "honest relish of balls and plays"? For an introduction to this debate and a balanced contribution to it, see the Bath chapter in Maggie Lane's *Jane Austen's World* (Carlton, 1996) or Paula Byrne's article "'The Unmeaning Luxuries of Bath': Urban Pleasures in Jane Austen's World" (*Persuasions* 26, 2004). For an illustrated account of Austen's time in Bath, see *Jane Austen in Bath: Walking Tours of the Writer's City* (Little Bookworm, 2006), by Katharine Reeve, a Bath local.

For more on Bath itself, we recommend two books: Peter Borsay's *The Image of Georgian Bath* (Oxford, 2000) and Graham Davis and Penny Bonsall's *A History of Bath: Image and Reality* (Carnegie, 2012). Both books explore how the city crafted and maintained its reputation as a premier resort town.

A CHRONOLOGY OF
JOHN MATTHEWS

Oct. 30, 1755: John Matthews baptized

Feb. 14, 1772: Matriculates at Merton College, Oxford

Nov. 9, 1778: Marries Elizabeth Ellis

1780: *Eloisa en Dishabille* published

1781–1783: Serves as physician at St. George's Hospital, London

1782: Receives his M.D. from Oxford

1782: "Ode to Cloacina" published

Sept. 30, 1783: Becomes a fellow of the Royal College of Physicians

April, 1784: Inherits the bulk of Elizabeth Skinner's £80,000 estate

Aug. 23–5, 1784: Delivers the Goulstonian Lectures at the RCP

Nov. 5, 1788: Begins construction on Belmont, his country seat

1793: Serves as mayor of Hereford

1794: "A Sketch, from *The Landscape, a Didactic Poem*" published

1795: "Bath: An Adumbration in Rhyme" published

1798: Founds the 1st Herefordshire Volunteers, a militia corps

1803–1806: Serves as Member of Parliament for Herefordshire

1812: His son Charles Skinner Matthews, a friend of Byron, drowns

1820: *Fables from La Fontaine* published

1825: Nationwide financial crisis results in the collapse of his bank

Jan. 15, 1826: Dies, aged 70

A CHRONOLOGY OF
JANE AUSTEN

1768: Austens move to Steventon

Dec. 16, 1775: Jane Austen born

1783: Educated by Mrs. Cawley at Oxford and Southampton; contracts typhus and is sent home

1785-1786: Attends Abbey Girl's School, Reading

1787: Begins writing her juvenilia, chiefly poems and satirical stories

1795–1799: First major creative period: completes early drafts of *Sense and Sensibility*, *Pride and Prejudice*, and *Northanger Abbey*

1800: Father gives up his living as rector of Steventon; family moves to Bath

1801–1806: Lives in Bath

1803: Sells the copyright to *Northanger Abbey* (then titled *Susan)* to publisher Benjamin Crosby, but he chooses not to print it

Jan. 21, 1805: Father dies; in the following years, Austen, her sister, and her mother change their lodgings several times

1809: Settles at Chawton Cottage, Hampshire on the estate of her brother Edward Austen Knight

1809–1816: Second major creative period: revises early novels, writes *Emma*, *Mansfield Park*, and *Persuasion*

1811: *Sense and Sensibility* published

1813: *Pride and Prejudice* published

1814: *Mansfield Park* published

1815: *Emma* published

Jul. 18, 1817: Dies, aged 42

1817: *Northanger Abbey* and *Persuasion* published posthumously

A NOTE ON THE TEXT

"Bath: An Adumbration in Rhyme" appeared in only one edition, which was printed in Bath itself in 1795. Our copy-text is held at the National Library of Scotland (catalog number: NE.20.h.14(14); ESTC N16155) and is used here by permission of that institution. It is a twelve-page pamphlet in quarto. The price of the pamphlet, printed on the title page, was one shilling (see the original title page on p. viii of this volume).

Reproduced exactly, the 1795 text would likely seem archaic and even a bit messy to modern readers. It uses the long 's' throughout, which newcomers to eighteenth-century texts often mistake for an 'f', and many words are capitalized or italicized according to conventions that are no longer observed. Indeed, the poem is not always internally consistent, either: at various points the city of Bath appears as "BATH," "Bᴀᴛʜ," and "Bath."

In most cases, we have chosen to follow modern conventions when doing so would render the poem more accessible to modern readers. Little of substance has been lost in the process: Matthews is a frank writer whose humor and meaning rarely depend on the placement of a comma or the capitalization of a word. The main changes to the original are as follows:

- The long "s" has been replaced with the short "s."
- Spelling has been modernized. For example, "stile" has been changed to "style."
- Contractions have been expanded except when the contraction is in current use or when expanding it would alter the meter of the line. Thus, "renown'd" has been changed to "renowned," but "you'd" and "ev'ry" have been preserved.

- Italics have been abandoned. Matthews uses the technique prolifically – sometimes to highlight a punchline, sometimes to express irony, and sometimes for little discernable reason at all. For a modern reader, the overall effect is somewhat fatiguing, and we have thus converted his italics to regular typeface throughout.
- Only proper nouns and the first words of lines and sentences have been capitalized.
- Punctuation has been modernized. However, we have preserved any comma that appears to mark a dropped syllable in the meter, as in the line "Sure such honor as this, must make a man vain." Here, the third foot ("must make") is one syllable short of an anapest. When reading the line, the reader naturally pauses over this missing syllable, a pause that is helpfully flagged by Matthews' comma, even if it is not strictly grammatical by modern standards.
- Spaces have been added between some lines to indicate changes of scene and other transitions.

BATH:
AN ADUMBRATION IN RHYME

Qui capit, ille facit.[1]

Of all the gay cities in Britain renowned,
Dear Bath is the place where most pleasure is found.
There alone is true breeding, politeness, and ease;
You have nothing to do but each other to please.
There the circle of day is one scene of delight,   5
From morning to noon, from noon until night;
For if dull in the morning, you open your eyes,
You may run to the Pump Room[2] as soon as you rise,
Where with puffing and blowing and hard catgut[3] scraping,
The town waits[4] endeavor to set folks a-gaping   10
(For the doctors all say, the waters to pass,
You should hear a brisk tune between ev'ry glass).
So the beaux in their boots, the belles in their slippers,
Come to walk up and down, and peep at the dippers,[5]
For though strange it appears, I'd have you to know,   15
Whilst you're drinking above, some are bathing below,[6]
And each glass of water brought up by the pumps
Contains the quintessence of half-a-score rumps.[7]

Having there drank enough, to banish the spleen,[8]
You go home to breakfast with appetite keen;   20
But as strong tea is apt to give people the vapours,[9]
After that 'twill be proper to read the newspapers,
To behold where your own name appears in the list
Of arrivals at Bath,[10] where Sir Sawny MacTwist,

"The Pump Room," *The Comforts of Bath*, Thomas Rowlandson, 1798. Yale Center for British Art, Paul Mellon Collection. Public domain.

[1] *Qui capit, ille facit*: A common epigraph for 18th-century satires. Literally, "The one who understands [these things] does [them]." More colloquially, "It takes one to know one."

[2] **Pump Room**: A fashionable gathering place in Bath. Visitors typically attended the Pump Room in the morning to meet friends and drink the waters, which were thought to have curative properties.

[3] **catgut**: Material derived from the dried intestines of livestock that was used to make strings for musical instruments.

[4] **town waits**: Local musicians whose duties in Bath included greeting visitors and providing live music in the Pump Room.

[5] **peep at the dippers**: Located above the King's Bath, the Pump Room offered guests upstairs a convenient view of the bathers below.

[6] **some are bathing below**: Visitors to Bath would bathe in the town's famous hot springs for health and leisure.

[7] **each glass… half-a-score rumps**: The water served in the Pump Room was not actually drawn from the baths below, though satirists often alleged it was.

[8] **spleen**: Low spirits, gloominess.

[9] **vapours**: A passing nervous affliction such as hysteria or melancholy.

[10] **list… Bath**: The Bath newspapers listed recently arrived guests in order of prestige.

If you met someone agreeable at a ball, the morning visit to the Pump Room was the first opportunity to see them again. After meeting Mr. Tilney, Catherine arrives at the Pump Room the next morning in high hopes of improving the acquaintance. Later in the novel, Isabella lingers in the Pump Room with similar intentions after dancing the previous evening with Tilney's elder brother.

Sir Walter Elliot learns of his cousin Lady Dalrymple's arrival in town from a Bath paper. It is no surprise that the class-obsessed Sir Walter has been studying the list of arrivals.

And Lady O'Connor, with Mynheer Van Prow,[1]   25
All figure away in the very same row.
Sure such honor as this, must make a man vain,
And chase all the megrims[2] that trouble his brain.

When you've with politics done, the beauties to meet,
You may stroll for an hour up and down Milsom Street,[3] 30
Where the misses so smart, at ev'ry fine shop,
Like rabbits in burrows, just in and out pop,
Where, booted and spurred, the gay macaronies,[4]
Bestride Mandell's counter[5] instead of their ponies,
Preferring the pleasure of 'tending the fair,   35
To breathing the freshness of Lansdown's pure air;[6]
Besides, "'tis the tippy"[7] and more in the flash,[8]
To canter away in the school of old Dash.[9]

Next on the parades you must walk for a while,
Then to lounge at the pump again is the style;   40
For at Bath, goddess Trivia has 'stablished her throne,
And even pleasure is managed by rules of her own,
And her laws are so good that 'twere pity to break 'em,
So there's appointed two priests, to make people keep 'em.
Them her Masters of Ceremony Folly here calls,   45
Who preside o'er the concerts, the assemblies, and balls;
The one is named Tyson, the other called King,[11]
Who wear each a gold medal, tied fast to a string:
On grave Tyson's bright bauble, Minerva is seen,
But on King's (much more proper) is Beauty's fair queen;[12] 50
For wisdom with fashion can never be found,
But too often with folly does beauty abound.
Now leaving these gents their official possessions,
We'll return to our subject and quit all digressions.

Let's haste to the Crescent,[13] that gay promenade,   55
Where many appointments and parties are made,

[1] **MacTwist… O'Connor… Van Prow**: Stereotypical Scottish, Irish, and Dutch names, respectively. Bath satirists often joked about the city's many foreign visitors.

[2] **megrims**: Migraines.

[3] **Milsom Street**: A fashionable street featuring shops and fine lodgings.

[4] **macaronies**: Foppish, overdressed men.

[5] **Mandell's counter**: The milliner Elizabeth Mandell sold ladies' hats and accessories from her Milsom Street shop c. 1788-1799.

[6] **Lansdown's pure air**: Lansdown Hill was a popular scenic destination nine miles from the city proper. Matthews jokes that the soft, foppish Bath bachelors are too lazy to attempt a ride of that distance.

[7] **the tippy**: The height of fashion.

[8] **in the flash**: Dashing or flashy.

[9] **school of old Dash**: Jonathan Dash (d. 1800) operated the main riding school in Bath during the 1790s. Evidently, the Bath gallants ride mainly for show, preferring a short trot around the local riding school to a real excursion.

[11] **Tyson… King**: Richard Tyson (1735–1820) and James King (1752–1816) were Masters of Ceremony, responsible for welcoming guests to Bath, making introductions, and organizing public amusements.

[12] **gold medal… fair queen**: The Masters of Ceremony wore official medallions for their roles as Arbitres Elegantiarum, or "judges of style." Tyson's featured Minerva, goddess of wisdom, while King's featured Venus, goddess of beauty and love. Matthews considers Venus the more appropriate patroness for Bath, a city of much beauty but little wisdom.

[13] **the Crescent**: The Royal Crescent, a semicircular row of houses in Bath and a fine example of Georgian neoclassical architecture. Also a popular place to walk.

Austen gives us an aged, subtler version of the macaroni in Persuasion. *Sir Walter Elliot is described as effeminate and conceited: "few women could think more of their personal appearance than he did."*

John Thorpe, Catherine's first suitor in Bath, offers to take her to Lansdown Hill in his gig, no doubt hoping to show off his driving skills.

The Masters of Ceremonies were also informal matchmakers. Catherine and Henry are introduced to one another by Mr. King during a ball at the Lower Rooms, with what success the reader of Northanger Abbey *already knows.*

"The Macaroni," Philip Dawe, 1773. Kunstbibliothek, Staatliche Museen zu Berlin. CC-BY-NC-SA.

Where fusty old maidens,[1] to look like the Graces,[2]
With well-padded bellies[3] and well-painted faces,
With many an ogle, a simper and smile,
Attempt the soft heart of some swain[4] to beguile: 60
But cease, wretched dotards, your weak arts to try;
How dare ye expect it, when Philips is by?
When Herring is near, how few can succeed?
By Salter's bright eyes, how many must bleed?
And brisk little Willis,[5] behold her who dare,   65
Of her sly roguish looks I'd have them beware.

Having paraded the Crescent full two hours or more,
For our dinners 'tis usual to part about four,
In eating and dressing, employ 'till near nine,[6]
And then to the ball to repair it is time: 70
That scene of enchantment, so truly divine,
Where mortals, like angels, transcendently shine.
To attempt to describe it, I fear, is in vain;
So much beauty on all sides, quite turns my weak brain;
But I'll muster up courage and banish my fears,   75
For who can be silent when Witham appears?
In the minuet[7] so graceful, who'ere sees her move
Must than marble be harder or else he must love.
When the Gubbins' advance, arrayed with each grace,
You'd swear they were daughters of Aether's soft race.   80
And Browne's[8] diamond eyes, armed with love-piercing darts,
Whenever they're seen, wound a hundred fond hearts.

The minuets o'er, see the crowd how it presses,
What havoc is made on the ladies' fine dresses!
Distinction of rank in a moment is gone,   85
And all eager for tea[9] in one mass now move on;
E'en the peeresses' selves, for whom benches were kept,[10]
Angry with the torrent, impetuous are swept;
And Mistress O'Darby, the dealer in butter,
Now sweats by the side of the sweet Lady Flutter,   90
Who would certainly faint, but her senses so nice

[1] **fusty old maidens**: Satirists often joked that spinsters came to Bath to hunt for husbands.

[2] **Graces**: Three beautiful daughters of Zeus representing the higher pleasures of life.

[3] **well-padded bellies**: In the 1790s, some women wore cushions under their dresses to create a more rounded figure.

[4] **swain**: A young lover.

[5] **Philips… Herring… Salter… Willis**: These names have not been traced and may be satirical inventions.

[6] **nine**: Public balls actually began shortly after six or seven, depending on the venue. Matthews may be mocking the excessive time some visitors spent dressing.

Mrs. Allen, Catherine's chaperone in Bath, is one such fastidious dresser. Her lengthy preparations cause Catherine to arrive late to her first ball.

"The Ball," *The Comforts of Bath*, Thomas Rowlandson, 1798. Yale Center for British Art, Paul Mellon Collection. Public domain.

[7] **minuet**: The more precise and formal of the two types of dance held at public balls, the other being the country dance.

[8] **Witham… Gubbins… Browne**: Young ladies who frequented the public assemblies. Honora (d. 1807) and Mary Gubbins were Irish sisters known in Bath for their musical talents; Honora was also a reputed beauty.

[9] **eager for tea**: There was a break for tea between the two rounds of dances at public balls.

[10] **benches were kept**: Seats at the head of the room were reserved for titled ladies.

In the tea-room, the gentlemen served the ladies. While intended to promote gallantry, the custom could create difficulties for unaccompanied women. At Catherine's first ball, she and Mrs. Allen sit awkwardly until a male stranger finally offers them tea. Henry's company at later balls offers many advantages, not the least of which is guaranteed access to the refreshments.

Are supported by smelling fat Alderman Spice,
Whilst his Worship's white wig almost smothers the face
Of her dainty young cousin, the dear Lady Grace.
The Countess of Pharo is forced to huddle   95
Between Doctor Squirt and his niece, Miss Di-Puddle;
Sir Stephen Newmarket, Sir Simon Profuse,
The Ladies St. Larum, and old Madam Goose;
For Commoners now, so saucy are grown,
That Cabbage the tailor, Lady Tombstone,   100
The Duchess of Basset, and Marquis de Frieze
All bundle together in one loving squeeze.[1]

Arrived at the tea room and compliments past,
Behold them sat down into parties at last:
But the tea-table-chat, so fully is known,   105
'Tis scarcely worthwhile by the Muse to be shown.
There's such a damned noise, and such a cursed clatter,
A bawling for sugar, for cream, and hot water,
None seem very anxious a long time to stay,
But just swallow their tea, and hasten away;   110
For the young ones, allured by the fiddle's brisk notes,
Make their mothers and aunts, near scald their old throats;
So many a character 'scapes being dissected,
And scandal, for once, is for dancing neglected.

Country dance,[2] of all others, best pleases the fair,   115
When the belles and the beaux so agreeably pair,
When each lovesick nymph,[3] may hear her dear swain,
In whispering murmurs, declare his sweet pain,
Where the sigh, and the smile, and the soft gentle squeeze,
All contribute the hearts of each other to ease;   120
Where no prudish aunts,[4] through old-maidenly spite,
Can hinder these symptoms of youthful delight.
But stop, my rash pen; it is time you should cease.
'Tis dangerous to dwell on such subjects as these.
For if, presumptuous, you venture to trace   125
In the maze of the dance, who moves with most grace,

"Inconveniences of a Crowded Drawing Room," George Cruikshank, 1818. Minneapolis Institute of Art. Public domain.

[1] **Distinction of rank… one loving squeeze**: In this scene of social confusion, tradesfolk and nobility are swept up in a universal rush for tea. The individual names are satirical. Lady Flutter has sensitive nerves. Alderman Spice is pungent, and Doctor Squirt, Miss Di-Puddle, and Sir Simon Profuse appear to be sweaty. The Countess of Pharo, Sir Stephen Newmarket, and the Duchess of Basset are gamblers: faro and basset were card games involving high stakes, and Newmarket was the center of English horse-betting.

Austen was familiar with the tea-room crush. At Catherine's first ball, she "is continually pressed against" as the crowd shoves its way through the tea-room doors. That this same company has just been dancing the stately and graceful minuet heightens the comedy of the moment.

[2] **Country dance**: The second type of dance performed at public balls. As Matthews implies, the country dance allowed for more conversation than the minuet. This was due to the simpler steps and the fact that couples spent much of the dance standing still as other couples completed their movements.

Catherine and Henry have "little leisure for speaking" during their first dance (a minuet), but they enjoy a long conversation during a country dance at a later ball.

[3] **nymph**: A beautiful young woman.

[4] **prudish aunts**: Chaperones to the young ladies. Matthews mocks them as killjoys, but chaperones and guardians played an important social role in distinguishing promising suitors from fortune-hunters and rakes.

In Austen's novels, proper guardianship is essential for young female visitors to Bath. Sixteen-year-old Eliza, Brandon's ward, is seduced and abandoned by Willoughby after being given the run of the town by her too-permissive host.

You will find it a task not so easy to tell:
It's an art wherein beauties so many excel.
But yet, I should hold you not a little to blame,
Forgot you to mention the charming Miss Vane,   130
The Butlers and Hamilton, Vassal and Mays,[1]
So justly entitled to share in your praise.
But proceed ye no further: there's so many more,
If you told all their names, you would scarcely give o'er
Until your ill rhymes to volumes would rise.   135
Pray stop where you are! "A word to the wise."

And yet, there are ladies of precedence grand,
Who of course have a right, the top-most to stand[2]
That might think their high titles not duly respected,
If their Honors' performances here were neglected;   140
So as it's our wish with all sides to keep well,
Proceed we their feats of the ev'ning to tell!
The Countess of Crab, having called the first dance,
Nimbly foots it away, with young Captain Prance,
And old Lady Sharpshins, who stands the next set,   145
Is wafted along, by Colonel Curvette;
A beau bonny Scot, with true Highland pace,
Next trips o'er the boards, with dear Lady Grace,
And the last of the fair ones with Nobles who number,
Is amused for the night, by Major O'Blunder.[3]   150

But the ballroom's so hot, 'tis stifling to stay,
So now to the cardroom[4] let's hasten away!
See old Mistress Macardo and Counsellor Gabble,
Young Colonel Mushroom and Alderman Dabble,[5]
At whist down together most lovingly sit;   155
Was ever a party so happily met?
The first who, though toothless, her pray'rs never said,
A lawyer the next, who a brief never read,
The third, a field officer,[6] just out of the cradle,
And the last, an old beast, who lives but at table.   160
So hum-drum the rest of the card parties seem,
That worthy of notice we do not them deem.

[1] **Miss Vane… Butlers… Hamilton… Vassal… Mays**: Young ladies who frequented the public assemblies and perhaps lived in town. Vassal, for example, is likely Elizabeth Vassall (1771–1856), daughter of an American loyalist who resided part of the year in Bath. Miss Vane may be Henrietta Vane, later Lady Langham (c. 1773–1807), a beauty and an heiress who also resided in Bath and married there in 1795. These catalogues of beauties were common in Georgian resort satire: the modest heroine of *Evelina* (1778) is scandalized to learn that she has been praised in one while visiting Bristol Hot Wells.

[2] **a right… to stand**: For country dances, ladies and gentlemen formed two rows; ladies of rank were entitled to stand at the head of their row.

[3] **The Countess of Crab… Major O'Blunder**: Satirical names. The Countess of Crab and Lady Sharpshins are unattractive, older ladies of rank: a "crab" or "crabapple" is a sour, inedible fruit, and "sharpshins" may suggest scrawniness. Their partners are fortune-hunting officers who appear to be sprightly dancers: "prance" and "curvette" both allude to fancy steps performed by trained horses. In Bath satires, wealthy but ugly women are often courted by good-looking but penniless men, particularly officers.

[4] **cardroom**: At public balls, cards provided alternative amusement for those unable or disinclined to dance.

[5] **Mistress Macardo… Alderman Dabble**: Satirical names, though the joke is not always apparent. Colonel Mushroom, as his name implies, is too young for his rank. Counsellor Gabble apparently chatters incoherently (gabbles), a possible joke on the legal profession.

[6] **field officer**: Officer in the army holding the rank of colonel, lieutenant colonel, or major.

Austen may be mocking the convention of the "catalogue of beauties" when she tells us that Catherine, during her debut in the Rooms, excited no "rapturous wonder" and was not "once called a divinity by anybody."

"The Successful Fortune Hunter," Thomas Rowlandson, 1802. The Met, The Elisha Whittelsey Collection. Public domain.

Mr. Allen heads "directly to the card-room" upon arriving at a public ball. His gout and his taste for political conversation both explain his preference for cards over dancing.

So now humbly we hope you will not think us rude,
If our efforts to please, for this time, must conclude,
Though much more of the rooms,[1] the concerts, and play   165
'Tis true, if he chose it, the poet might say.
But as through one day of folly you've safely been led,
He'll wish you good night and retire home to bed.

Entrance and Façade, Upper Assembly Rooms, Bath.
Photograph by Mark Anderson, 2005. CC-BY-SA-2.0.

¹ **the rooms**: The Upper and Lower Assembly Rooms, the two main venues for public balls and concerts. The ball described in this poem takes place at one of the two. In their heyday, the Upper and Lower Rooms attracted a varied company, from the nobility down to the minor gentry. As more tradespeople began frequenting the Rooms, however, some members of the upper crust began to seek out other venues.

Austen seems to have been fond of these inclusive venues, where guests could mingle regardless of class and wealth. Naturally, her more snobbish characters despise them. Anne Elliot's relatives shun the Upper and Lower Rooms, preferring the "elegant stupidity of private parties."

Tea Room, Upper Assembly Rooms, Bath. Photograph by Charles DP Miller, 2012. CC-BY-SA-2.0.

Printed in Great Britain
by Amazon